Six-Word Lessons on
GROWING UP
AUTISTIC

100 Lessons to Understand how Autistic People see Life

Trevor Pacelli

Published by Pacelli Publishing
Bellevue, Washington

Six-Word Lessons on Growing Up Autistic

Published by Pacelli Publishing
9905 Lake Washington Blvd. NE, #D-103
Bellevue, Washington 98004
PacelliPublishing.com

Cover and interior designed by Pacelli Publishing
Author photo by Holli Dunn Photography

ISBN-10: 1-933750-29-4
ISBN-13: 978-1-933750-29-3

One percent of the population of children in the U.S. aged 3-17 have an autism spectrum disorder...

One in 68 newborns will be born with an autism spectrum disorder...

Only 56% of students with autism finish high school...

One million Americans live with an autism spectrum disorder...

My name is Trevor Pacelli. I was diagnosed with Autism at age 5. I am the first in my extended family to have autism. Growing up autistic has been difficult not only for me but for my parents and my sister. We've all had to learn about autism and how to maintain a peaceful household. I deeply want other families with autistic children to learn from my experiences. This is why I wrote ***Six Word Lessons on Growing Up Autistic.***

In ***Six-Word Lessons on Growing Up Autistic,*** you will find 100 short, practical tips to help understand the autistic person in your life, told through insightful personal experiences by someone who has grown up autistic. Rather than pore through pages and pages of content, ***Six-Word Lessons on Growing Up Autistic*** gives them to you quickly and easily.

My hope is that you are able to use my experiences to help you with raising your autistic child, or relating to anyone you know who is living with autism. Tell me how it's impacted you at Trevor@GrowingUpAutistic.com.

For my sister, Briana, for understanding me when no one else did.

For my Mom, Patty, for helping me write and edit this book.

For my Dad, Lonnie, for encouraging me to write this book.

And for my Auntie Lori, who is now with her Savior.

Table of Contents

Suspecting that your Child has Autism

1

Other children don't act like yours.

Some first clues that a child has autism are the differences from other children. A few of these clues are: delayed speech, not understanding what you are communicating, crying when held, advanced abilities and obsession in a specific area, such as, for me, putting together puzzles.

The doctor has the right voice.

"I'm sorry to tell you this, but your child has autism." It's scary to hear this coming from the doctor when your child is first diagnosed. Your pediatrician is a good first step for finding specialists who will help with a diagnosis. The doctors should be honest, even if it contradicts what you want to hear, or what your friends are telling you.

Some don't like to be hugged.

Children with autism like to have their space, and that means they sometimes dislike having people in physical contact with them. Although it's not true in my case, many autistic children feel very strongly about being held, touched, or hugged.

Speech is an important early sign.

According to my pediatrician, by age two, a child should be speaking at least two words to form an idea. If not, this is a good reason to suspect autism. This was the case with me, and I immediately began work with a speech and language pathologist, to help me learn to comprehend as well as communicate better.

Do they ever make eye contact?

Children with autism are often more interested in the texture of the furniture than they are in you, so they may not make eye contact with you. However, they are very observant, so they will notice everything, including your attitude toward them.

A child's mannerisms are quite distinguishable.

Does she sway when she walks? Is her posture leaning a certain direction? An autistic child can have physical habits that make her stand out. These habits can be managed with physical or occupational therapy. I appreciated it when people kept in mind that it was still part of my identity.

They may interact differently with siblings.

Most parents have multiple children, and when they are young, the kids are together much of the time. If one of them has autism, he may have a more difficult time getting along with his siblings. Work with his siblings to help them understand your autistic child's differences and needs, especially for time alone.

They very rarely share their thoughts.

You may think they are being secretive and simply not sharing. But I have this issue all the time as well, and I can say that usually these children are just really protective over what fantasies go on in their head.

They don't like to be disturbed.

Because autistic children are not very open with their thoughts in the real world, they can't stand when people try to break the barriers in their heads. Until they learn better coping skills, they will most likely cry, scream and get upset with their parents when interrupted.

New places often make them cry.

Leaving the house for a new place can intimidate autistic children. Because they are not familiar with anything, they will complain about wanting to go home. To prepare for this, bring something like a favorite toy, and give plenty of advance details about the outing.

They play very well by themselves.

My mom tells me that I was actually easy to take care of when I was very young, because I loved playing by myself. I could stay focused on my favorite activity, puzzles, for hours, and didn't need any attention. This was very different from my sister, who demanded a lot of interaction from a parent or other child.

A Different View
of the World

You won't believe what they think.

Most people think in logical terms, others think in imaginative terms. But some who have autism, such as myself, think in completely abstract terms that makes little sense to others. It is a combination of imagination and how they see things.

They don't just see a tree.

Instead of just seeing a tree, they may add on to that and imagine it painted pink and yellow, sprouting seventeen eyeballs and growing to Godzilla height. Their imagination lets them see everything as a world of their own.

Their imagination is over the top.

A grapefruit peels open and a hybrid giraffe-bat comes out and sings *Mary Had a Little Lamb* in Chinese. That is just an example of how my imagination functions. Anyone other than me would not understand where I got this.

15

They observe everything to the extreme.

With my case of autism, I have a very strong attention to detail, for I notice little things that other people do not. Others like me also have this, and it has been shown that most autistic people are extremely visual learners and observers.

They find it tough to explain.

With all that is happening in my head, I sometimes cannot find it in me to share any of it with others. My thoughts are very personal to me, and I usually just can't form thoughts into words.

17

Only focus on one single subject.

Because I get so focused and absorbed into whatever I am doing, it often takes a full hour to fully move on from that activity to another. This is one reason transitions are one of the most common difficulties for autistic people.

It's difficult to try new activities.

I have certain subjects, such as drawing and art, in which I'm very fascinated. When I was younger, I actually had an aversion to any other subjects or interests that were not my own, and often did not want to join in such activities.

19

They have their own exceptional talents.

With myself, I know that I have a true gift in drawing and photography. Every autistic child is not artistic, but they usually have a specific exceptional talent that stands out. One may be a whiz in history, a master in marine biology, or even a careful nutritionist!

They get either As or Fs.

With some autistic kids, their brains allow them to do either tremendously well or horribly. One may be a master in science and just breeze through all the labs, but just cannot perform a math equation to save his life.

21

Nobody on earth thinks like them.

I have met very few people who have the same wide-ranged, detailed thinking style that I possess. Every individual who has autism has a unique way of thinking, which can provide help in areas that no one else can.

Time Alone Versus Time with Others

Most autistic kids need time alone.

I have always felt that having time by myself helps me to unwind and smell the petunias. But this doesn't mean I'm antisocial. I still enjoy the company of friends and family, just not as much as most people.

Some actually prefer to be alone.

While I do not necessarily always want to be alone, I still feel much more sustainable with myself and able to unleash my emotions when I'm on my own. Others who are like me may also feel happier when alone.

Balance solo activities with parental interaction.

While it was easy for my parents to leave me alone to play when I was young, part of my speech and language therapy was for them to actually play with me and talk to me in specific ways that taught me to communicate better. It just needs to be balanced with the needed time alone.

25

They also want to go out.

In high school, even though I needed time alone, hanging out with people outside of school was my main desire. I felt very envious whenever I saw my friends hang out with others and felt a powerful urge to fit in with everyone else.

They need to vent their problems

Some may have to explain what's troubling them immediately to others. But it has always been important to me to have some time alone for a while to reflect over what is bothering me before expressing it verbally.

27

Getting out helps their social skills.

I can name times I have been out with friends and said things that have hurt someone's feelings. But getting out and being with friends helped me to be more aware of other people's reactions and emotions.

Everyone needs to be socially active.

If everybody avoided socializing and never left their house, then the world would be a terribly boring place! Every human who has ever lived--even those with autism-- has his piece to fill in this giant puzzle known as society.

Some can have sudden mood swings.

One minute, they love talking to others. Then suddenly, a painful memory comes up in their heads and they no longer want to speak. I always have this happen to me and it certainly affects how I react around others.

They can function properly when alone.

Whenever I am by myself, I feel like I can think more about whatever is going on in my life. If I am around a huge crowd for an extended period of time, I can't properly process all the overwhelming activity.

31

On vacation, they need alone time.

For any age, whenever visiting relatives, sightseeing, or going out for extended periods of time, they need time away from others to be on their own. I still feel the need for occasional times alone while I'm out on vacation.

Sudden Changes are a Big Challenge

Beware of them throwing a fit.

When I was much younger, I often cried and fell to the ground every time something unexpected happened. Even if it was a trip to the zoo--something kids would usually be excited about--I felt really strongly about it because it wasn't expected.

They plan out their entire day.

I personally function best when I plan my day, which means planning what I am going to do and for how long. This is why I feel so strongly about sudden plans that interfere with my schedule throughout the day.

They can't transition between things easily.

As I have said, it is difficult for me to move from one activity to the next. I can only make a smooth transition in a proper setting that accommodates what I'm doing along with enough support to push me through.

Their brains need time to process.

Although I am better now with sudden schedule changes, I still need some time to process the thought before I can go along with the change. That's really all that most autistic kids need to calm them down: time.

36

Reactions can come out as unexpected.

You say to your autistic child, "We're going to the park to play Frisbee!" but your child may just cry and whine. Although they usually love going to the park, they just weren't ready to go right at that minute.

They like to set a schedule.

I always wake up at a certain time, shower at a certain time, and have a set time to go to sleep every day. I rarely go out of this routine and this really helps to keep my mind stable.

They dislike not getting their way.

It's not necessarily, "my way or the highway," but rather, "I was ready to have this happen to me, not something else." I'm so ready for one thing to occur that when the opposite happens, I become unhappy.

Learning new things is really hard.

For those who have autism, it can take at least twice as long or more to learn something new. They are not used to anything unfamiliar, and don't really want to feel forced to apply something new to their life.

Surprises aren't such a good idea.

One thing about people with autism is that they can be so lost in their own little world that they are incredibly sensitive to anything unexpected. Surprises such as sneaking behind their back to intentionally startle them or other teasing usually upsets them.

41

Just think patterns. Just think patterns.

My daily life follows a pattern: Get up, go to class, go home, do homework, and go to bed. Anyone with autism would follow a similar pattern. Once the parent notices this as well, they will better understand the child.

Getting Out There
to Make Friends

Time with friends versus time alone.

Everybody has to get out there and be social with people, right? But if someone has autism--at any age--they need to learn to balance needed and desired friendships with time alone, which I need to unleash my emotions and unwind from the worldly pressures.

43

They don't know what to say.

Some people with autism have difficulty forming into words what exactly they are trying to tell someone. I still have this issue. The idea is in my head perfectly, but forming it into words is difficult and takes time.

Getting to know people is difficult.

I can clearly say that for autistic people, it is really hard to find something they have in common with others. Since their attention is not fully on the person, they don't know what to say or do while around them.

45

They can't explain what's bothering them.

Again, people with autism don't know how to explain their thoughts. If you ask them what's bothering them, they will most likely say that they are not sure what it is. But in reality, they just don't know how to explain it.

They don't know how to react.

While out with people, there are a lot of things that other people may say to an autistic child that he is not sure how to take. Innocent statements that may not offend others may offend him. Comments that may seem clear to some may be confusing to an autistic child. As result, he may not know how to respond to some things others may say to him.

Jokes may be taken too literally.

While I've never had a problem with taking things literally, I know other kids with autism have an issue with mishearing some jokes that others tell. This can lead to them feeling confused, amazed by a sarcastic comment, or offended.

Insults may be taken too personally.

Whenever someone says something to me that intends to hurt my feelings, I feel very down on myself and at the bottom of the world. I, along with several others like me, have very sensitive emotions that get hurt easily.

Autistic children have trouble sharing thoughts.

While out with friends, what drives the social event is everyone sharing their experiences. But that one person with autism just can't share her thoughts to the others. She is afraid of sounding either unusual or too different from the crowd.

50

Their words can come out wrong.

Again, I have this problem all the time. I say something one way and it comes out entirely different without me even knowing. As a result, others' feelings get hurt, or they may think I am being rude or snappy.

51

There's always the feeling of loneliness.

This is something I have had to deal with my whole life; seeing my friends going out with their closer friends, and never asking me to join. Seeing that from anyone's eyes can be enough to bring down their spirits. Keep encouraging your child to not give up, and they will find some true friends.

What is the Best Schooling Option?

52

Early intervention is an important step.

Start as young as possible visiting various doctors to find out your child's needs and getting an exact diagnosis. I was diagnosed with speech and language delay at two and began private therapy with a speech pathologist. This helped prepare me for finding the right preschool.

53

Diagnosing autism leads to better opportunities.

At age five I was diagnosed with Pervasive Developmental Disorder-Not Otherwise Specified, a type of autism. Because of this, I qualified for special services in my public school and was placed on an IEP (Individualized Education Program) from kindergarten through high school.

Individualized Education Programs help track learning

With the diagnosis of PDD-NOS, I was given the right to be placed on an IEP, which meant that I had a special education teacher assigned to my case, who met with my parents and worked with my other teachers to set and track goals for areas such as academics, behavior and communication.

School options for the elementary years.

My parents took advantage of the special services offered at my public elementary school. Your particular child though may fit at certain types of private schools such as Christian, Montessori, or special needs centers that work with autistic children.

If there is no verbal communication.

In this case the choices are a bit more limited. Based on the child's learning ability, it could be more appropriate for you to teach him. But there are other options, such as private schools and tutors who can communicate and teach in a way he can understand.

57

Consider how they interact with teachers.

Teachers are the main mentors of your child growing up. With autism, a child may love one teacher, but feel uncomfortable with another. For me, the top priority of my learning and school experience was being comfortable with the person teaching me. The best teacher could be a parent.

Is making friends always a priority?

There might be a time during your child's school years where social skills should become a lower priority than academics. For me in seventh grade, making friends was less important than working in a productive learning environment, so I began home-schooling.

Transitioning between schools can be difficult.

Because of the difficult transition between elementary and middle school, my parents decided to homeschool in middle school. For two years, I took classes at my public school, lessons at home with my parents, and classes at a smaller homeschool center. There are many options to consider when finding the right fit for your child.

Any schooling option can be changed.

My school career switched from public school to homeschool, then back to public school in ninth grade, which was right for me. While autistic children like pre-dictability and consistency, don't look at any schooling decision as one that must continue until graduation.

Transitions in School as they Age

61

Teachers can make a big impact.

I was blessed to attend school in a good public school district and am thankful for the many caring teachers, principals, counselors and others who had good knowledge of how to work with autistic children, and had love, care and concern for me. Great teachers combined with parent involvement helped me to learn and grow, both academically and socially.

The teachers are not always terrific.

There were also a few teachers along the way who did not fit my learning style. Work with the administrators to find the best teachers who fit your child's needs; being involved with parent teacher organizations and helping in class will help get to know teachers as well.

Every grade's harder than the last.

There's a reason why each grade is given a number; it shows the increasing difficulty, which is especially noticeable for autistic children. Get to know the teachers and stay involved with your child's homework so you can help your child advance from each grade to the next.

There's that unexpected amount of homework.

For autistic students, anything that is more than expected is very difficult. Because they like their life to be the same every day, homework duties are especially difficult. Work with the teacher to help your child know what to expect.

Every school has a big bully.

Autism can make your child a target of the school bully. Keeping in clear communication with your child, as well as his teachers and other parents will help you know what's going on, and help control the bullying.

They may fall under the influence.

Some autistic kids may not have the right judgment when offered drugs or alcohol. Is taking these pills bad? Is what this kid is saying about cigarettes being "not so bad" true? Be very specific when explaining substance abuse to your child.

New schools mean meeting new people.

Going to new schools, whether middle school, high school or college has been hard for me because of all the new unfamiliar students. I can take as long as six months to connect with friends, and even longer to know who my real friends are.

Switching schools is hard to do.

When I started going to college, everything became more difficult because I was in a new location with new people and a new learning style. It is challenging for others like me to make this big of an adjustment.

Being away from parents is difficult.

When your child goes to college, he or she might be away from you. They take longer than others to accept that they're apart from their parents, and need extra help to get over the negative feelings of extreme separation.

The subjects are beyond their interests.

All students are required to attend classes they consider boring, in which they have little or no interest. An autistic child would not be as accepting of this, because they are even more narrow and obsessive about the things about which they are truly interested.

They walk from class to class.

As I've said earlier, some like me can focus only on one single subject. College could clearly be a frustrating time slumping from class to class on a large campus, and the amount of work, all from different classes, can be overwhelming.

Major Life Events are Especially Challenging

72

Moving starts a whole new chapter.

In their old home, a child knew where everything was, but in a new home, he suddenly can't find anything and has to start all over with his daily activities and routines. Let him know beforehand where all of his personal items will be so he will feel more comfortable with the new house.

73

It's a boy! It's a girl!

I am the youngest in my family, so I never had to experience having a little sibling. For autistic children who have to adjust having a new baby brother or sister, take extra care to prepare him for what to expect, and give him an even mix of separation and one-on-one time with the other sibling.

"Daddy won't live with us anymore."

While divorce devastates everyone, it is especially hard for your autistic child because it upsets his orderly world. If divorce happens, try to maintain his routine as much as possible, and give him plenty of advance details about visiting schedules and any other changes at home. Help him stay in contact with the other parent with social networking, phone, and Skype, depending on his age.

"Daddy has a new wife now."

As if divorce wasn't bad enough for your child imagine if her mom or dad got remarried to someone else! Try to be accommodating when the child requests time with her biological parent. The adjustment will take time and patience. Keep your autistic child informed of plans and developments so she is not surprised.

The parent's new partner moves in.

When it comes to divorce, your child may have no choice but to live with the divorced parent's new partner. This is a major challenge for an autistic child. To make it easier, work with both your partner and child to get to know each other better and explain how the new arrangement will work.

77

The new partner brings in siblings.

There is a chance the new partner may bring in sons and daughters of her own, requiring your autistic child to adjust to stepsiblings at home. Spend extra time helping the stepsiblings learn about autism and your child's specific challenges. Look for things they have in common, and help them get to know each other.

The nanny is here. Now what?

If you are planning to hire a nanny, introduce your child to her several times beforehand, and let her join you for dinner several times. Make sure the nanny familiarizes herself with autism and your child's needs before starting the job. Schedules and routines will be helpful for everyone involved.

The older sibling must move on.

I had to let my sister go when she left home to attend college. The instant I realized she was gone, it was difficult for me to accept. But in time, I got used to it. It helped to know when I would see her again, whether she was coming home, or we were going to visit her. We also kept in touch through Facebook.

Relatives who stay for much longer.

Every now and then, you may have relatives staying at your house for an extended time. This could upset your child's daily routine and involves unfamiliar people, so help him get to know the relatives by filling him in about them before they arrive. Let the relatives know how to relate to your child as well. If they must sleep in his room, provide a space where he can create a temporary routine with his own things.

Forgiving and Forgetting About the Past

They hold on to their grudges.

Looking back ten years ago, I am still annoyed at someone for either hurting my feelings or simply being an annoying pest. For other kids with this problem, they should be reminded about the more friendly people they know today.

Guilt gets the better of them.

Realizing my wrongs brings down my spirits tremendously throughout the day. If your autistic child has this issue, clearly explain that what they did wasn't so bad compared to what other kids their age often do in the same situation.

Their memories are sharp and vivid.

With some autistic people, such as me, their memories are so precise that they remember the little details in a situation that others do not. Keep this in mind while encouraging your child to put those painful memories behind him.

A situation can make them opinionated.

Your child may feel strongly about a certain viewpoint, which could originate from a past experience he had. This experience could change the way he sees everything today, so help your child focus on the true current issues.

They often keep track of people.

If your child has a problem with tolerating someone they consider intolerable, help him organize a T-chart for that person-- one side for the person's good qualities, the other for bad qualities. This helps give your child a more realistic viewpoint.

It is hard to forget negativity.

Having a narrative look on life, I find it difficult to let the past go because it made me who I am today. Work with your child to see that it is okay to remember the past, but not overly dwell on it.

They'll look back and feel bad.

Remember that one time your child broke the cookie jar fifteen years ago and you scolded him? Well, because of his vivid memory, he is still mentally scarred by the painful memory. It is important to be understanding if he feels bad about past experiences.

Feelings are too sensitive to forget.

Whenever I get an emotion, whether it is laughter or sadness or anger, it is more extreme than everyone else's. Your child will need you to help him talk through these emotions and keep them in perspective. Validate his feelings, but show him other viewpoints as well, keeping in mind his vivid memory.

They take things much too personally.

Someone may insult your child, either intentionally or unintentionally, and he will take it much harder than others would, keeping him from socializing with anyone. He really needs to hear your encouragement to stay away from negative thoughts.

Overreacting often results in negative thoughts.

Reflecting upon all the bad things I've done in the past has made me vulnerable to feelings of self-hate and worthlessness. Solutions may require anything from counseling, positive encouragement, or, when younger, simply distracting him with an activity to take his mind off of things.

Daily Dealing with your Autistic Child

How they'll interact with your friends.

Parents of autistic children are often concerned about how their child will present himself to your friends, knowing that he may say something inappropriate. Try to anticipate each situation and remind your child specifically how to interact with guests each time.

You'll hear new stories every day.

Many days, your child may come home from school feeling overwhelmed by the busy, difficult environment. Be patient with starting after-school activities and have an open ear to hear what your child might want to tell you about his day.

They don't feel sharing is caring.

I have never liked to share my personal interests or thoughts, because I felt they were too different from everyone else. For your child, help him to bring out those thoughts once in a while rather than all at once.

Relationships are not always a priority.

Many autistic people would rather spend time inside their minds instead of with others. It is your duty as a parent to bring your child out of his comfort zone and aid him in engaged conversations with people he knows.

They are sensitive to almost everything.

Whether it is touch, sound, sight, taste, or smell, a child with autism is sensitive to anything extreme. This is when it's always good to have something such as a stress toy or hug machine to help him calm down.

Get their siblings on their side.

Your nonautistic sons and daughters can help your autistic child overcome daily pressures. Keep them just as educated about the autistic child as you are, and perhaps even let them read this book. This will benefit them when they get older.

Phone a therapist-they can help!

I've talked with a therapist who specialized in working with teenagers with autism, who showed understanding and helped by talking me through my struggles and concerns. Ask your child's school counselors for recommendations if you think your child needs an outside counselor.

Give them time
on their own.

Being out with so many people for too much time creates a very overwhelming atmosphere for your child. So, if at any time, he says he needs some time by himself, give it to him; because it does help him.

Give them patience, let them think.

If something comes up suddenly for me, I don't know how to take it. If I am just given about fifteen minutes to mull it over and process the thought, I can be more reasonable about accepting the change.

100

Put love as your top priority.

While growing up, my parents always made sure I knew they loved me. This helped significantly in bringing my spirits up. Every day, tell your child you love him, but not too much, or he will feel uncomfortable with you.

More books on Autism
Available on **GrowingUpAutistic.com** in paperback and e-book

50 Things You Should Know About Me
by Trevor Pacelli

The Kindergarten Adventures of Amazing Grace
by Briana Pacelli

Six-Word Lessons for Autism Friendly Workplaces
by Patty Pacelli

Six-Word Lessons for Dads with Autistic Kids
by Lonnie Pacelli

Six-Word Lessons on Females with Asperger's Syndrome
by Tracey Cohen

Connect with Growing Up Autistic

Facebook.com/GrowingUpAutistic
Twitter: @GrowingUpAutism

About the *Six-Word Lessons Series*

Legend has it that Ernest Hemingway was challenged to write a story using only six words. He responded with the story, "For sale: baby shoes, never worn." The story tickles the imagination. Why were the shoes never worn? The answers are left up to the reader's imagination.

This style of writing has a number of aliases: postcard fiction, flash fiction, and micro fiction. Lonnie Pacelli was introduced to this concept in 2009 by a friend, and started thinking about how this extreme brevity could apply to today's communication culture of text messages, tweets and Facebook posts. He wrote the first book, *Six-Word Lessons for Project Managers*, then started helping other authors write and publish their own books in the series.

The books all have six-word chapters with six-word lesson titles, each followed by a one-page description. They can be written by entrepreneurs who want to promote their businesses, or anyone with a message to share.

See the entire *Six-Word Lessons Series* at **6wordlessons.com**

98445324R00070